Teaching Left-Handed Children

Margaret M. Clark

Hodder and Stoughton
London Sydney Auckland Toronto

Published with the cooperation of
the Scottish Council for Research in Education

ISBN 0 340 18199 0

Printed and bound in Great Britain for
Hodder and Stoughton Educational,
a division of Hodder and Stoughton Ltd,
Mill Road, Dunton Green, Sevenoaks, Kent,
by Biddles Ltd, Guildford, Surrey

Contents

	Page
Preface	5
Introduction	7
Developmental aspects of laterality	9
Ambidexterity	10
Eye dominance	11
Crossed laterality	12
Inheritance of left-handedness	13
Mirror-writing	14
Stuttering and left-handedness	23
Laterality and reading difficulties	25
Incidence of left-handedness	28
Left-handedness and writing problems	30
Conclusions	45
References	46

Preface

The first edition of this book* was published in 1959 at a time when a more permissive attitude to left-handedness was becoming apparent in schools. That edition contained the main findings of the author's research into left-handedness, prepared in accordance with the Scottish Council of Research in Education's policy of making the results of educational research available to as wide a public as possible.

It is a matter of some concern to the author that though at the present time left-handed children are now allowed to use their left hand for writing, yet in all too few instances are they taught how to use it. It is hoped that this second edition, *Teaching Left-Handed Children*, which provides an up-to-date summary of research on left-handedness relevant to education and an outline of the basic considerations in the teaching of writing to left-handed children will prove of interest and help to teachers, parents and others dealing with left-handed children.

* *Left-handedness: Laterality Characteristics and their Educational Implications*, 1957. Publications of Scottish Council for Research in Education, XXXIX, University of London Press.

Introduction

Right-handedness is not a single factor existing in almost the entire human race with only one or two exceptions termed left-handed; nor can hand dominance be adequately described in terms of a dichotomous classification of right- and left-handedness appearing in unequal proportions. In short, differences in the proportion of right and left dominance are apparent not only in the total population, but also in the same person for different activities, the preponderance of right preference being greatest in those activities most connected with school writing. The number of persons showing consistent preference for one hand or the other appears also to vary for different activities and to be greatest in the more skilled and more often practised tasks.

Lateral asymmetry is a feature not only of use of the hand, but also of foot, ear and eye. The presence of a connection between the preference of foot and hand has been noted, and the lack of connection between those of hand and eye. The association between the ear preferred in listening and the preferred eye, when the subjects were unaware that either of these aspects was being tested, has also been noted.

Writing difficulties of left-handers and the analysis of their writing as compared with that of right-handers is a subject of some practical importance. The absence of a significant difference between the speed or quality of writing of the left-handers and right-handers reveals only the probable absence of a general connection. Though left-hand writers are not inevitably slower or poorer than right-hand writers as a result only of using the left hand, the conclusion should not be drawn that there are no left-handers whose writing is suffering either in speed or in quality. Some valuable information might be secured by an investigation of the relative scores of a larger number of older left- and right-handers on such single aspects as speed, legibility, quality, pressure, and, possibly most important of all, fatigue from long periods of writing.

Developmental aspects of laterality

There is ample evidence to show that both hand and eye preferences are established in almost all children prior to school age, which discounts the view that the school writing situation is the first indication of right-handedness in the majority, and which negates the opinion that some form of rebellion against school authority is an explanation of left-handedness.

Ambidexterity

Mention might be made of a cult at the beginning of this century initiated by Jackson (1905) who founded the 'Ambidextral Cultural Society' for the promotion of educational reform and two-handed training. Jackson even advocated that children should be trained to use both hands simultaneously in writing, and, as a final step, taught to write different things with both hands at the same time. His book *Ambidexterity* is a rather extravagant but entertaining advocacy of the benefits to be derived from becoming equally skilled with both hands. As a result of Jackson's work many infant schools introduced two-handed training and copy books were even prepared for this, but the craze did not survive long. Its main interest now is that it accounts for the view held so often by people of a certain age-group that ambidexterity is the ideal.

Eye dominance

Here also the incidence found varies with the criterion and the number of tests and whether preference for one eye or the other is being measured, or dominance of one when both eyes are acting together. The percentage of left-eyedness found is somewhere between 25 and 35 per cent depending on the number of tests used, and well over one-third of the population shows some left preference (see Clark, 1957, and Kellmer Pringle, 1966). In one of the recent studies where a marked increase in left-handedness was found, there was no evidence of either an increase in left-eyedness or a sex difference (Clark, 1970).

Crossed laterality

If approximately one in ten of children is left-handed and one in three is left-eyed, then it can easily be appreciated that a considerable proportion of children must have preferred hand and eye on opposite sides, that is, be crossed laterals.

Inheritance of left-handedness

Genetic studies have revealed that the development of handedness preference has a hereditary basis; in other words, one's chances of being left-handed are greater if there are instances of left-handedness in the family. Few would deny, however, that factors other than genetic help to determine whether any particular individual will be right or left-handed: the actual society in which he lives and its attitude to left-handedness, other environmental factors, temperamental differences, and so on, all play a part in determining whether latent left-handedness will be cultivated or suppressed. These factors will probably have their greatest effect on the intermediates, assuming left-handedness to be a quantitative trait. The environmental variants probably account for the slow progress which has been made in formulating an adequate and satisfactory theory concerning the actual mechanism of inheritance. The increase in apparent left-handedness in the last generation, and also the fact that so many institutions, schools and clinics make a note of the handedness of entrants, should assist geneticists in their attempts to determine the actual hereditary mechanism operative in hand preference.

It is still difficult, however, to obtain reliable information on handedness over more than one generation, which makes it difficult to determine the precise genetic mechanism. As the incidence of left-handedness varies from place to place, time to time, and even for different tasks within the same individual, it is difficult to obtain sufficiently precise information. It seems unlikely that a genetic mechanism is the complete explanation.

Mirror-writing

Definition of mirror-writing

Mirror-writing is the term used to describe writing which appears normal only when reflected in a mirror. The term usually refers to script in which the mirror-image is produced laterally—that is, the type in which all the letters and words are correctly formed in reverse and the whole proceeds from right to left, since other types are extremely rare. It has been found that some people have a peculiar facility for producing such writing spontaneously even without previous practice. The most famous of such persons was Leonardo da Vinci, whose notebooks were written in mirror-script. Another example is the 'Looking Glass Writing' illustrated in figure 1, which Lewis Carroll used when writing to some of his young friends.

The inclusion of this phenomenon in a study of left-handedness is justified by the fact that almost without exception mirror-writing is produced either by left-handed persons, or, at least, by use of the left hand. It has been established that Leonardo da Vinci drew with his left hand, and this can be verified from the manuscripts where it is clear that the lines and shading were performed with the left hand, as also was the mirror-writing, as may be seen in the photograph on page 17. Controversy has arisen as to whether da Vinci was natively left-handed or whether he only used his left hand as a result of paralysis of his right arm with which he was afflicted in later life. Contemporary writings indicate that he did in fact use his left hand even as early as the age of twenty. Lewis Carroll is known to have stammered, and it is suggested by Burt (1937) that he may have been a changed left-hander.* The two examples cited above reveal that mirror-writing may be found in highly intelligent persons. It has been shown by Gordon (1921), however, that its incidence is much higher among the mentally defective than in the normal population. Fragmentary mirror-writing even with the right hand is actually found in some children in the early stages of writing; this is understandable when one considers that there is nothing absolute about a left to right direction, and that in fact in some countries writing does actually proceed from right to left. Fluent mirror-writing is actually a left-hand production, for reasons which will be discussed below.

Explanation of mirror-writing

The most natural direction for movement with either hand is away from the body; the normal direction of our western writing is accordingly from left to right, which is the natural direction of movement with the right hand. In early times, in Greece for example, the mode was for a time left to right and right to left on alternate lines, with the actual letters reversed in the right to left line. Some investigators have suggested that leftward writing, as for example in Hebrew and Arabic today, may be indicative of predominant left-handedness, but they have not considered the fact that it is only in our type of continuous, flowing writing, where

* It is easier to track down left-handers among artists than among writers, since, even when forced to use the right hand for writing, artists who have a strong left-preference will probably use their left hand for drawing and painting. This may even be seen in children who, when forced to use the right hand for writing, still draw and even rule lines with the left.

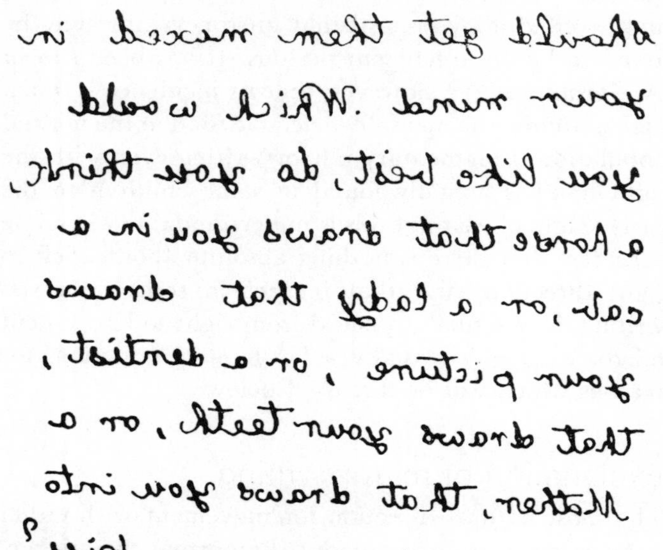

should get them mixed in your mind. Which would you like best, do you think, a horse that draws you in a cab, or a lady that draws your picture, or a dentist, that draws your teeth, or a Mother, that draws you into her arms, to give you a kiss? And what order would you put the others in? Do you find Looking-Glass writing easy to read? I remain your loving Lewis Carroll.

Figure 1 Extract from a Letter in Mirror-Writing by Lewis Carroll taken from *The Life and Letters of Lewis Carroll* by S. D. Collingwood

By courtesy of the Director of the Science Museum, South Kensington

A Page from the 'Notebooks' of Leonardo da Vinci illustrating his use of Mirror-writing

the characters are joined, that one direction, namely the outward one, is favourable. For the left hand the movement away from the body, the easier movement, is from right to left; thus if there is no inhibiting factor, either visual or intellectual, or if this is temporarily removed, the left hand may produce mirror-script. It has been suggested that the transfer of training produced by teaching the right hand to do normal writing is towards mirror-writing with the left hand, at least in the absence of visual cues. Few left-handers have until recently been permitted to use their left hand for writing when at school, which would have impressed the left to right direction and inhibited mirror-script. Their spontaneous writing with the left hand, therefore, remains mirror-wise and is one explanation of the considerable facility with which some adults can produce mirror-writing. This facility will probably become less common in left-handers except among those who are forced to write with their right hand, since the practice in the left to right direction which the left hand will receive in producing the normal writing will inhibit it, while it will probably become more common among left-handed children in the early stages of learning to write. It is accordingly important that those in charge of children should be aware of the explanation and causes of mirror-writing so far as these are known, and that they should know how to prevent and treat cases which they do encounter.

Mirror-writing is not a sign of mental deficiency, though its prolonged occurrence is common in mental defectives. This is partly explained by the greater number of mental defectives who actually use the left hand for writing, and also by the absence of the factors which lead to its disappearance in a normal child. The realisation that he is actually producing a type of writing different from that produced by others, and unintelligible to them, is necessary in the left-hand writer before he will be prepared to change. Such a realisation will be dependent on a certain level of intelligence, perceptual ability and vision. In short, though an intelligent left-handed child may produce mirrored letters or words in the early stages more frequently than does a right-handed child, visual cues and comparison with the writing in books will lead to the realisation that his writing is in some way different, and will suggest a correction of the tendency; but such a realisation may not be present in a dull child. Probably if teachers were aware that a right to left direction in writing may be normal to a left-handed child and may be attempted by him, they could by suitable methods prevent the habit from developing. As individual schools and districts began to permit children to write with the left hand, the teachers were seldom aware of the difficulties, such as those mentioned already, which might be encountered by the left-handed child. Another problem is this unconscious feeling for writing out from the body, which when encouraged with the right hand gives the correct direction, but which with the left is incorrect. Lack of understanding of this may result in some teachers giving instructions or demonstrations which may encourage rather than prevent mirror-writing.

Spontaneous mirror-writing is not actually a very frequent occurrence in the normal child, though the potential ability to produce it is present in many left-handed adults, usually those who normally write with the right hand. The actual percentage of mirror-writers found in the school population has varied with the criterion adopted, since one may either ask the teachers to note all children who have ever produced mirror-writing, or only those who produce it under experimental conditions. The figure given by Burt (1937) is about one in five hundred children, while the figure quoted by Gordon (1921) is 0·48 per cent in the ordinary elementary schools and 8 per cent in schools for mental defectives.

The most effective force in the prevention of mirror-writing is probably vision. Some children are evidently not aware that this type of writing in any way differs from the normal, since they can, in fact, read the product.* Others who produce mirror-writing are unable to read their product, but do not see that it is different because they are also unable to read ordinary writing, an inability which may be due to low intelligence or to a specific reading disability. The idea that all people can be classified into visiles, audiles and motiles, and that learning is predominantly or completely of one type has been abandoned in recent years, and few hold the view that teaching should be directed through different sensory modes for different children. It does, nevertheless, remain true that certain individuals are more affected by, and employ, visual stimuli to a greater extent than other sensory stimuli, whereas others are more inclined to learn by touch. It is probable that mirror-writers are among the latter type, since the feel of the writing is correct in mirror-script. This suggestion was discussed in great detail by Burt (1937):

> *As the mirror-writer forms his letters, the correctness of the particular shapes and the wrongness of the general direction seem alike attributable to the fact that the nervous centres for motor control and the nervous centres for visual*

* Monroe (1932) has suggested that mirror-reading, that is, the ability to read mirror-script or tendency to read mirror-wise, may be connected with left-eyedness rather than left-handedness (pp. 87-8).

control may at times function in total independence. With nearly all of us, immediately an action becomes completely automatic, it tends to slip away from the control of the attentive eye, and to be left to the half-conscious guidance of the muscle-sense (p. 345).

With the guidance of the 'muscle-sense' the result would be correct, provided the person were using the right hand, but when the hand used is the left, this reliance results in mirror-writing.

Prevention of mirror-script

Mirror-writing in the early stages does not present great difficulty, if handled correctly. The teacher should be aware that such a tendency may be potentially present in a left-handed child, particularly if he is more motor than visual in his learning. Mirror-script proceeds in a leftward direction, and can thus only be produced when the person commences at, or towards, the right hand side of the page. To prevent such writing one must use some device to ensure that a potential mirror-writer always starts at the left of the page. This may be done by marking the starting place with a cross. If a child is nevertheless found to be producing mirror-writing thereafter, it may be necessary to stop all free writing for a time, and allow only slow careful writing from a copy until a rightward direction has been developed. Tracing over letters may also assist provided that the starting place is marked and that vision is emphasised as a further guide to the correct direction.

There is nothing normal about the one direction of writing and abnormal about the other. It should be remembered that in some countries it is the leftward direction which has to be cultivated. It is true, however, that some people have greater difficulty than others in accustoming themselves to the rightward direction of western writing. Mirror-writing does not necessarily have pathological significance, and its appearance in a left-handed child in the early stages of learning to write is not a matter of great concern, provided steps are taken to prevent it from becoming a habit. Only when it continues in an older child as his only, or usual, form of writing is it likely to be associated with mental deficiency. It most commonly accompanies left-handedness and nervousness or lack of attention, though the lack of attention may actually be concentration on some other aspect of the writing, speed for example. In conclusion, it is most important to remember that one should not regard or appear to regard it as a sign of mental retardation. Parents and teachers who adopt this attitude are creating in the child an emotional 'set' and a feeling of nervousness, which is just the type of situation in which mirror-writing is produced unconsciously, while the emotional 'set' may even develop into hostility and result in a negative attitude to all school work.

Stuttering and left-handedness

Certain limited conclusions can be drawn from the volume of research which has been carried out on handedness and its relationship to stuttering.

1 Changed handedness does not always result in stuttering. The fact that stuttering does not result in those who require to change from the preferred hand because of some accident is evidence that there is no absolute relationship between the two.

2 Stuttering may result from changed handedness, but whether it does or does not will depend to a great extent on the procedure adopted in effecting the change. The stuttering is not, however, a direct result of the change, in the sense that some upset of the neurological balance causes abnormal speech; rather it is a possible manifestation of emotional disturbance resulting from the resistance by the child to the attempts to make him conform against his will to the wishes of the majority.

3 Certain periods appear to be critical with regard to speech development, and attempts to change handedness at these ages may have adverse effects on speech. It would seem to be desirable for the child to develop dominant handedness as early as possible, and any action which may delay that should be condemned, though, here again, the retarded speech and delay in acquiring dominant handedness may both result from some deeper neurological inadequacy.

4 All children have not the same tendency to develop a stutter even when the environmental circumstances are comparable; in children whose 'tolerance' is small, a

change of handedness will accordingly have a considerable effect and may even act as the precipitating factor. There may be some weakness of the speech mechanisms in potential stutterers; this implies that while in such people stuttering is the reaction to extreme emotional circumstances, in others the reaction may be enuresis, or squinting—in each instance the weakest link.

It is clear that to gain a complete picture of stuttering attention must be paid, on the one hand, to the physiological aspects of the problem, in the form of a possible weakness or inadequacy of speech functioning, with a probable hereditary basis: and, on the other hand, to the psychological aspects, in the form of emotional stresses which precipitate the stuttering in a particular instance. Only among such stresses would changed handedness be included, and even then only as one possible precipitating factor. Undue emphasis of one aspect, such as changed handedness, is thus to be deplored.

Recent studies do not support the view that stuttering is a psychological disorder, but that in certain families there may be a predisposition to speech difficulty of which stuttering may be a manifestation. A survey of children with a stutter and a comparable group of the same age showed no evidence of an excess of left-handedness or of changed handedness in the stutterers (Andrews and Harris, 1964). There is some evidence of an association between delayed development in skilled use of one or other hand in otherwise intelligent children and defective or slow speech development. It is not clear, however, whether there is a causal relationship between these, or whether both are the result of a third common factor.

Laterality and reading difficulties

Reading backwardness and laterality

Since 1930 there have been many studies of reading backwardness in which attention has been paid to the possibility of a connection between left-handedness and left-eyedness or crossed laterality and reading difficulty. For a summary of the conflicting evidence in these early studies see Clark 1957 pp. 100-105. A number of these early studies were carried out on clinic populations or on very small numbers. In a series of large-scale surveys since that date there has been no evidence of an association between reading progress and any aspect of laterality preference—either hand or eye—or indeed of crossed laterality. In a recent population study reported in *Reading Difficulties in Schools* (Clark 1970) some of the precautions necessary before drawing any conclusions from the incidence of left-handedness in any group of backward readers is discussed in some detail (see also Hillman, 1956, and Douglas, Ross and Cooper, 1967). From the present evidence it would appear that the emphasis placed on left-handedness as a possible cause of backwardness in reading in courses for teachers was misplaced.

Remedial work and laterality

There was *no* evidence of a differential rate of improvement with remedial work associated with any type of laterality in a study by Cashdan (Cashdan, 1967).

Fernald, famous for her remedial work, observed as early as 1943 that

the right-handed cases and the cases of matched eye-hand dominance resemble the cases in which the dominance is not matched, are as serious in their deficiency, learn by the same methods, and are as successful in the final outcome. The eye and hand dominance is not changed as a result of the remedial work; that is, the subject with unmatched eye and hand dominance learns to read and is able to read in an entirely normal manner with eye and hand dominance opposite (p. 150).

Hand preference and prediction of reading progress

Attempts which have been made to predict children's progress in reading on the basis of their early hand preference have been unsuccessful. De Hirsch, for example, in 1966 described in her book *Predicting Reading Failure* her attempts with young children to ascertain which tests would be predictive of later reading difficulty—left-handedness was not one.

It seems unfortunate that there has been a failure to draw the attention of parents and teachers to these findings.

Recent studies tend to show that what is important for reading is not which hand or which eye is dominant, but rather whether or not the child has developed laterality and directionality. . . . Difficulties in laterality and directionality tend to be regarded by neurologists as indicators of either defect or immaturity of the brain centres. With or without neurological basis, improvement is possible with special training (Harris, 1966).

26

Lack of dominance and reading difficulties

While there is no evidence in recent surveys of an association between reading progress and hand or eye preference there remains the possibility of a connection between failure to develop dominant handedness and delayed speech possibly associated with later reading difficulties (Ingram, 1960). There may be forms of reading backwardness in which such failure is a characteristic. There could, however, be a further more fundamental weakness causing the slow development of hand preference, the delayed speech and the reading difficulties. This is, however, a field in which further study is required.

Directionality

The finding that confused directionality may have significance in cases of reading difficulties is important for the teacher as it draws attention to the importance of ensuring that the child acquires a consistent approach in the identification of words in reading. Reversals are common in many children in the early stages of learning to read and write. What is surprising is the failure of many teachers to appreciate the need to teach most children—whether left- or right-handed—the significant characteristics for the discrimination of letters and words. 'Directionality' is one feature which has not previously been significant for recognition of an object, yet this is important for discrimination of both letters and words.

Features of print significant for reading should be *precisely* specified to the child, whether he be left- or right-handed. To describe letters as being 'the same' or 'different' is *not* sufficient, the teacher must indicate which characteristics of sameness are important. *Directionality* is one crucial feature; while an aspect of difference which is not significant for reading is size of print.

Incidence of left-handedness

The present author in her earlier study (Clark, 1957, 1959) found that most left-hand writers had been subjected to a period of writing with the right hand and had only been permitted to return to left-hand writing when this was unsuccessful. It is seldom the case now that teachers prevent or actively discourage a left-handed child from writing with that hand. There are, however, many parents who would prefer their children not to show left-handed tendencies.

In studies of the incidence of left-handedness it is important to note the criterion of left-handedness used by the author. With the increased permissiveness towards use of the left hand for writing there is evidence of a greater incidence of left-hand writers in schools. In a recent study of seven-year-olds, the present author found 8·8 per cent were using their left hand for writing and more still might have been classified as left-handed had some other criterion been used (Clark, 1970). An increase in incidence has also been shown over a ten-year period in studies by the Scottish Council for Research in Education (S.C.R.E., 1963, 1968). The incidence of left-hand writers among ten-year-old boys was found to have increased from 6·8 to 8·2 per cent and from 5·1 to 6·7 per cent in girls. In all large-scale studies a greater incidence of left-handedness has been found in boys than in girls. At one time it seemed plausible to explain this difference in terms of the greater susceptibility to social pressure of the girls. Had this been the explanation one would have expected that the proportion of left-handers in the two sexes would have become more similar as the social pressures to right-handedness were reduced. On the contrary the sex difference has remained as has the higher incidence of left-handedness in twins, though it is rare to find both twins left-handed.

In a large scale survey in the United States involving 92,656 children, Enstrom (1962) also found an increase in left-handed writers and a greater proportion of boys (11·1 per cent boys and 9·7 per cent girls) and no variation in incidence across school grades. Thus it is possible that we can anticipate a higher incidence yet of children using their left hand for writing and it seems unlikely that the sex difference will disappear.

Left-handedness and writing problems

Until recently only a minority of those with left-hand preferences were actually using the left hand for writing, though many of them were using it for almost every other skilled action. Some adults, even though forbidden to use the left hand for writing at school, after leaving school changed over to writing with the left hand of their own accord and rapidly acquired great facility.

The efforts to change left-handed children to the use of their right hand varied in strength from year to year, district to district, school to school, and even from one family to another. One of the most unfortunate aspects of the treatment meted out to left-handers was its inconsistency, not only from one child to another, but also with an individual child. What happened until recently was that in the infant classes, no objection was raised to the child using his left hand; but for nearly every pupil there came a stage in his school career—often about the age of eight at the time he should have been acquiring some speed in his writing—when a teacher suggested to the child, or insisted, that he try the other hand. Sometimes he was made to feel so awkward and different that he changed over of his own accord; a change for this reason was more frequent with girls than with boys.

Certainly a more permissive and tolerant attitude has developed over the years to the 'sinister' minority. Seldom are children in this country now forced or even 'encouraged' to use their right hand when the one they prefer is the left. Left-handedness is now sufficiently accepted that few glances are cast at the left-hand writer because of his strange way of writing. All this is true, and with this changed attitude, the incidence of left-hand writers has increased in recent years. Now, about one in ten young children at school writes with the left hand, with a marked excess of boys using the left hand (the proportions being similar in university students). However, it would seem that little progress has been made beyond that of permissiveness.

Luckily for left-handers, the fine, hard nibs and plain pens, so difficult for them to manipulate, are a thing of the past. With the improvement in, and widespread use of the ball-point pen one of the hazards has gone. It would appear that even now, however, little specific guidance in writing is given to left- or indeed to right-hand writers by teachers; perhaps not sufficient guidance is given to the teachers! Simple adjustments which would make writing so much easier and less tiring for left-handers are seldom allowed and more rarely actually taught.

Common characteristics of writing with the left hand

1 The actual writing

Most left-handers, given time, can write neatly; their most common failing is their inability to acquire the necessary speed to meet everyday requirements. This is not, however, a necessary characteristic of writing with the left hand, but only a failing commonly found as a result of lack of proper guidance. The slope of their writing is seldom naturally a forward slant, and where this has been insisted upon by the school, the slant frequently varies from letter to letter, and from page to page. No definite style is acquired; it is as if a left-hand writer were still seeking some new adjustment or more comfortable technique, even at the adult stage. The writing of left-handed children is often messy and when written in ink is frequently smudged. This is not so true of the adult left-hander who has usually developed some technique whereby this is avoided, but often success is attained only at the cost of considerable strain.

2 *Position when writing*

When writing is done with the left hand, an awkward position is frequently adopted. A cramped position of the arm and twisted position of the whole body is very common, as also is an awkward tense grip of the pen or pencil. Left-handers seem to remain conscious of the writing movement for a long time; they have accordingly jerky, effortful movements when writing. They use many odd methods of writing. A warning is nevertheless necessary in this connection, since those who write in an odd manner are those who are noticed, while other left-handers writing in a normal easy way are seldom apparent to the casual observer. Thus people are inclined to generalise from the few awkward left-handers they have noticed, and to assume that awkwardness is a characteristic of left-handedness. A considerable number of left-handers do, however, have some peculiar method of writing. This is true not only of adults who grew up at a time when left-handedness was even less tolerated than it is now, but is also true of young children in schools today.* There are various types of peculiarity in the way the pen is held, the commonest being 'the hook', where the hand is actually above the line of writing, as shown in figure 2 (*a*). In fact, this position

* This statement was originally written in 1959 but is still true today.

is so common that it is even regarded by many teachers as the normal method of writing with the left hand. There is nothing normal about this position, and some consideration of the differences between writing with the right and with the left hand readily explains how it develops. When one writes with the right hand, the hand is ahead of the writing; while to achieve this when writing with the left hand, the writing would require to be done from right to left. Thus a left-handed child finds when he starts writing that the grip which the teacher demonstrates and which his right-handed neighbour takes of the pencil is not suitable, and since he is shown no alternative, he adopts a grip of his own. He must so grip the pencil that he can see what he is writing; and he therefore grips it at the same distance from the point as does the right-hander, but curves his hand slightly to enable him to see under it. This device is fairly satis-factory with pencil writing, but when he begins to write with ink he finds it is no longer satisfactory for two reasons: first, the point of the pen pokes into the paper; second, continual smudging of the writing results, as the hand is still rubbing over the writing. Smudging may still result with a ball-point pen unless the grip is adjusted so that the hand is clear of the writing. The child accordingly completes the 'hook', placing his hand above the writing. This in turn is unsatisfactory though it is one adaptation which teachers seem to permit left-handed children to acquire. It is difficult to achieve neat writing by this technique and since it is also a continual strain on the hand anyone adopting it will readily become fatigued if required to do much writing. Another method used by left-handers is to turn the paper sideways and write down towards the body, this being another attempt to acquire a comfortable position. Teachers are inclined to correct this position, but seldom suggest an acceptable alternative. One child, pointed out as a neat writer though left-handed, was questioned as to his method of writing. It was found that he had no peculiar grip of the pen and fairly free movement somewhat similar to that of a right-handed child. On inquiry as to how he avoided smudging his writing, it was found that he used blotting paper after every word. The product was neat but extremely slowly performed and with considerable unnecessary labour. It should be noted that use of a ball-point pen does not always prevent smudging of writing if the child's hand covers previous written words. Cole (1934), who made a study of the development of these habits, found that the three types illustrated in figure 2 appeared frequently. Thus these are not isolated cases but are typical of left-hand writing positions.

Causes of the characteristics of left-hand writers

Not all of these characteristics are true of all left-hand writers, but they are typical of the writing and writing method of left-handed adults and children. Only by an analysis of the faults can one decide whether they are a necessary feature of writing with the left hand, when a transfer to right-hand writing might be the most satisfactory treatment, or whether they can be cured by a different technique of writing with the left hand, in which case reform of the teaching is the solution.

All the faults listed above could easily be prevented by some guidance in the early stages. *Writing with the left hand is not the same as writing with the right, with only a change of hand.* For the movement to be the same with the left hand the writing would require to be performed from right to left, as only then would the hand be

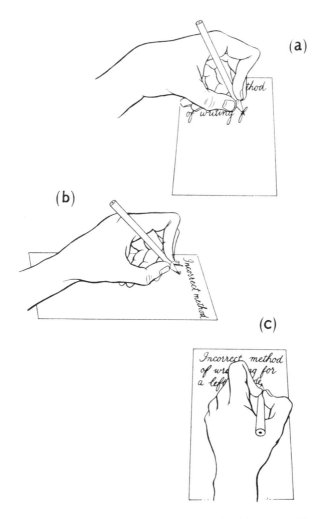

Figure 2 Illustration of Incorrect Writing Positions adopted by Left-hand Writers: (a) arm hooked above writing, (b) writing in towards body, (c) with arm cramped in to side

moving away from the body while progressing along the line of writing, as occurs with right-hand writing. In view of this, some adjustments are necessary, otherwise situations such as these already indicated develop and result in slow awkward writing. What is worse is the fact that by the time the person is old enough to be aware that his technique is uncomfortable and inefficient, it has become too stereotyped to be changed without great difficulty. In many schools pupils with a strong preference for the left hand are now allowed to use it for writing, but they are only *permitted* to write with the left hand and not *taught* how to. Usually the result is that they grip the pencil wrongly; they place the paper as for right-hand writing inevitably resulting in a cramped arm movement, since, while the right arm moves away from the body in writing, the left arm moves in towards and across the body.

It may be asked whether one need look and feel awkward when writing with the left hand, and, if not, why that does so frequently happen. Many have assumed that all these symptoms are typical of what inevitably happens when one writes with the left hand. This is, in fact, one of the excuses given for the insistence on writing being performed with the right hand.

It is now some years since investigators suggested that bad writing need not necessarily result from using the left hand and since constructive suggestions were made for the proper guidance of left-handers in learning to write. As early as 1927, West pointed out the need for a set of directions for dealing with the left-handed child.

> *There is a great deal of uncertainty among teachers as to what to do with the left-handed writer. Some proceed to make him over into a right-handed writer as expeditiously as possible. Others will do so only on condition that the*

child is below a certain age. Some will permit the child to write 'backhand' if it is natural for him to do so, others insist on the imitation of the formal slant. Definite and detailed recommendation is needed with regard to these and many other points bearing on the left-hand writer, the mirror-script writer, the subnormal, and the physically defective child. These pupils though in the minority, are often encountered, and the problems relative to their instruction are very confusing (pp. 55-6).

Cole, in 1934, in her book on the *Psychology of the Elementary School Subjects*, devoted considerable space to a discussion on the teaching of left-hand writers. As she pointed out:

If the left-handed child is independent enough to succeed literally single-handed in his contest with his teachers, some at least of whom will try to change him, his troubles have only just begun. All systems of writing are based on the assumption that the writer will use his right hand. The youthful and determined left-hander is usually forced into a system not in the least adapted to his needs (p. 122).

She then went on to state that the correct posture for the left hand is as comfortable and relaxed as that for the right. Orton, in 1937, also discussed the correct position for the paper and the writing with the left hand; while Freeman stated that the left-handed child is apt to acquire a highly awkward method of writing if left to himself, but if properly taught he may develop a habit of left-handed writing which is nearly as convenient as is right-hand writing. In 1939 Cole discussed in great detail all the points of importance in teaching left-hand writing, and also explained how the peculiarities in left-hand writing arise in the present system which is quite unsuited to their needs. In 1945 an instruction manual was published by Gardner to serve as a guide both to teachers and to adults who had developed inefficient writing methods with the left hand. The writer's aim in the manual is to assist left-handers to acquire an easy movement in writing, and by this means attain effortless, speedy writing. In the Editor's Foreword it is stated that it is the only manual which has been prepared specially for this purpose. The exercises are so planned that they can be used by the left-hander himself with a minimum of guidance.

These examples may suffice to show that material is available, and has been available for many years, on methods of teaching a left-handed child to write; any suggestions which are now offered have thus at some time been given by others, though the emphasis may be slightly altered. They are assembled here and repeated in the hope that their inclusion in a work specifically on left-handedness may direct to the basic essentials the attention of those actually concerned with teaching of writing to left-handers. The suggestions may even instil a new spirit into the whole work of handwriting instruction, basing it on greater awareness of the differing abilities of individual pupils, and directing it more to the writing needs of later life.

Suggestions for the teaching of left-hand writers

The following three improvements, if adopted and applied, would in themselves eliminate the awkward postures common in left-hand writers and make their writing movements smoother and less effortful.

Position of the paper

Authorities on handwriting instruction have for many years been contending that the correct position of the paper when writing with the right hand is at an angle, with the left-hand top corner of the paper nearer the body than the right. The reverse angle is correct when writing is performed with the left hand; in this case the effect of the wrong position is more unfortunate. If the paper is placed horizontally and directly in front of the person writing with the left hand several difficulties arise: (*a*) with the paper in the horizontal position a backward slope in the writing is easier, a regular forward slope being almost impossible; (*b*) as the hand progresses across the page the arm becomes more and more cramped in towards the body, whereas in right-hand writing, which is moving away from the body all the time, the movement across the page becomes continually freer; (*c*) it is very difficult to see what has been written as the hand covers the words, which of course also leads to smudging of the paper. Accordingly, from the early writing lessons a left-handed child should sit slightly to the right side of the desk, with the paper placed alongside him on his left, thus allowing a freer arm movement.

In this connection Gardner's manual gives the following instructions:

Now study the position of your paper. At the left end of the first line of writing, your pencil will start far to the left. As you finish at the right edge of the paper, your pencil will still be slightly left of the mid-line. This is the reverse of the movement used by the right-handed writer who starts to the right of the mid-line of the body and writes far to the right.

The paper should also be angled with the right-hand top corner of the paper nearer the body than the left (as in figure 3), the actual angle depending on the individual child and the slant of writing desired. If the paper is so placed, a freer movement develops; it eliminates the tendency to use the 'hook' movement,

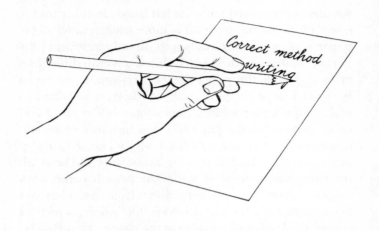

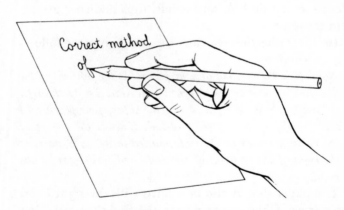

Figure 3 Illustration of Correct Position of Paper for Writing with the Left and the Right Hand

and it makes possible the development of vertical writing, or even a forward slant, without any strain. Many left-hand writers adopt this position of the paper themselves, but at the moment it is frequently done in face of the opposition of teachers who still insist on the central horizontal position of the paper.

Type of pen

Hard as it is for a right-handed person to write with an extremely fine nib, it is almost impossible for the left-hand writer, as the push and pull movement with the left hand does not permit the efficient working of the nib. It is essential that left-handed children should use broader and more flexible nibs than their right-handed fellows so that they will not be slowed up unnecessarily or caused to jab holes in the paper when writing. The most suitable type of nib is one with a slightly turned-up point, or one with a slightly bulbous end. It is possible to procure a nib cut with a reverse oblique point, which prevents the side being rubbed off the nib with continual use, a result that is apt to happen, especially with a fountain pen, where the nib is not changed frequently. Some, though not all, ball-point pens are also suitable for left-hand writers.

Grip of the pen

It is necessary when writing with the left hand to grip the pen or pencil at least an inch or even an inch and a half from the point, in order to keep the hand below and well clear of the stems of the letters, so that the child may be able to see what he is writing. This grip may also prevent him from smudging his writing, of which fear the right-handed child is free since his hand is usually alongside and to the right of the writing and consequently clear of it. A further precaution which is specially necessary with a left-handed child is to ensure that he does not grip the pencil or pen too tightly. This is a very common failing with all children when beginning to write; it causes tension and increases fatigue, but usually this grip is relaxed as the writing develops. Many left-handers, even adults, nevertheless clutch their pens in a vice-like grip and push hard in their attempts to write.

If, however, the nib is of such a type that it will work when guided across the page, without actual pressure having to be exerted down on the page, this difficulty will be overcome. Not all fountain pens or even all ball-point pens are easy flowing enough for a left-hand writer.

These three recommendations, on the position of the paper, the type of nib, and the grip of the pen, indicate the most important adjustments for the left-handed child, and they are also the simplest to apply. Various writers have stressed other points, for example, that the light should come over the right and not the left shoulder for the left-handed child so that his hand will not cast shadows on the writing. That is an adjustment, which, though desirable, would disturb the normal organisation of the class, and is only suggested as an additional, and not an essential, improvement.

Cole and Gardner have both suggested that left-handed children should have their first writing practice at the blackboard since this encourages a full arm movement with greater freedom and a less cramped position. It also prevents the development of any such odd grips as 'the hook', since the hand is of necessity below the writing. *Frequent* practice of *large* writing on paper should be provided. It is inadvisable to make the child write very small letters in the early stages when his muscular coordination is not yet sufficiently

42

developed for fine movements, as this results in tense-
ness and a tightening of the grip on the pencil. If the
child is allowed to do big bold writing at the start, it
will be found that as he develops better control, he
reduces the size of the letters of his own accord.
Economy was probably behind the insistence on small
writing even in the early stages; with this went insistence
on perfect formation of all the letters, which meant that
only a line or two of writing was achieved in a writing
period. As in many other skills, the character of the
skill changes as the writing is speeded up; this implies
that slow careful writing is not a training for speedy
legible writing. Elaborate curls and twists on letters
which can be achieved in slow writing are actually
detrimental to legibility when the writing is speeded
up; a simpler style would be easier to write and to read.
Gardner's manual for left-handers gives a series of
exercises for developing this simple easy flowing writing
at high speed without fatigue. These consist of groups
of similar letters to be practised repeatedly. Cole
mentioned similar exercises for the right hand, and
suggested that they should be practised at greater and
greater speed until they could be performed at a high
speed with no decrease in legibility.

*It is the object of these drills to establish rhythm, which is a
highly desirable element because it contributes to both speed
and ease of writing. Other speed drills consist of writing a
single sentence as many times on successive days as possible
(without diminishing the legibility) in a short period of
time—perhaps three minutes.*

In *The Backward Child* Burt pointed out:

*I have seen teachers going round a class, showing other pupils
how to place the paper and hold the pen, but leaving the
left-hander to discover these things entirely for himself.
Actually he needs more help, not less, if he is to learn how*

to manage his left hand efficiently. His paradoxical task is to produce with the left hand a style of writing evolved for the right. . . . There is, however, no necessity to describe in detail the requisite adjustments: they will be evident to the teacher after a little reflection, particularly if he first tries the experiment of left-handed writing himself.

In view of the types of fault which are still current among left-handers this policy of assuming that each teacher will know what to do and, what is more important, will do it, does not seem to be successful.

It is to be hoped that with the renewed interest in the teaching of handwriting and spelling as basic pre-requisites to effective written communication attention will be paid to the distinctive needs of right- and left-handed children. Though there are thousands of possible causes of illegibility in writing, yet within any one person's writing there may be only a few. Thus helping children to acquire speedy yet legible writing will require individualised instruction. Here, however, the support and cooperation of the other children in the class can frequently be enlisted and result in interesting, appropriate and individualised writing practice.

Instruction in hand-writing based on professional competence is as essential for the one in ten children who are left-handed as it is for the remainder whose preference is for the right hand.

Conclusions

Left-hand writers, as this study shows, represent only a fraction of those with left-hand tendencies. Some have been changed to the right hand, others have transferred of their own volition after commencing writing lessons, while still others have been changed even before entering school. The percentage of children using the left hand for writing seems to be increasing. Now almost one in ten of the children in school in Britain will be using their left hand for writing; more of the left-handers being boys than girls. It is imperative that the same attention be given to teaching left-handers to write with the left hand as is devoted to right-handers.

It is important that all those associated with the training of teachers focus attention on the importance of teaching left-handed children to write clearly, fluently and effortlessly. Finally students, teachers and parents should be made aware of the lack of evidence of failure to make progress in reading as a necessary or even likely concomitant of left-handedness.

Left-handedness has its disadvantages in a right-handed world, but even some of these disadvantages are slowly being rectified as machines are being produced with adjustments for use by left-handed operators, and as even scissors, potato peelers and tin openers have become available for left- as well as right-hand use.

References

ANDREWS, G. and HARRIS, M. (1964) *The Syndrome of Stuttering* Clinics in Developmental Medicine, No. 17, London: Heinemann.

BURT, C. (1937) *The Backward Child* London: University of London Press Ltd.

CASHDAN, A., PUMFREY, P. and LUNZER, E. A. (1967) 'A survey of children receiving remedial teaching in reading', *Bull. Brit. Psychol. Soc.* **67**, 17a.

CLARK, M. M. (1957) *Left-handedness: Laterality Characteristics and their Educational Implications* Publications of the Scottish Council for Research in Education, No. 39, London: University of London Press Ltd.

CLARK, M. M. (1970) *Reading Difficulties in Schools* Harmondsworth: Penguin Education.

COLE, L. (1934) *Psychology of the Elementary School Subjects* New York: Farrar and Rinehart, Inc.

COLE, L. (1939) 'Instruction in Penmanship for the Left-handed Child', *Elementary School Journal*, **39**, 436-48.

DE HIRSCH, K., JANSKY, J. J. and LANGFORD, W. D. (1966) *Predicting Reading Failure* New York: Harper and Row.

DOUGLAS, J. W. B., ROSS, J. M. and COOPER, J. E. (1967) 'The Relationship between handedness, attainment and adjustment in a national sample of schoolchildren', *Educational Research*, **9**, *iii*, 223-32.

46

ENSTROM, E. A. (1962) 'The extent of the use of the left hand in handwriting', *Journal of Educational Research*, **55**, *v*, 234-5.

FERNALD, G. M. (1943) *Remedial Techniques in the Basic School Subjects* New York: McGraw Hill.

FREEMAN, F. N. (n.d.) *Solving Handwriting Needs As We See Them Today* Columbus Ohio: Zaner-Bloser Co.

GARDNER, W. H. (1945) *Left handed Writing—Instruction Manual* Danville, Ill: The Interstate Co.

GORDON, H. (1921) 'Lefthandedness and Mirror Writing especially among Defective Children', *Brain* **43**, 313-68.

HARRIS, A. J. (1966) 'Child development and Reading', paper presented at the International Reading Association Conference in Paris.

HILLMAN, H. H. (1956) 'The effect of laterality upon reading ability', *Durham Research Review* **7**, 86-96.

INGRAM, T. T. S. (1960) 'Paediatric aspects of specific developmental dysphasia, dyslexia and dysgraphia', *Cerebral Palsy Bulletin* **2**, *iv*, 254-77.

JACKSON, J. (1905) *Ambidexterity* London: Routledge and Kegan Paul.

MONROE, M. (1932) *Children Who Cannot Read* Chicago: University of Chicago Press.

ORTON, S. T. (1937) *Reading, Writing and Speech Problems in Children* London: Chapman and Hall Ltd.

PRINGLE, M. L. K., BUTLER, N. R. and DAVIE, R. (1966) *11,000 seven-year-olds* London: Longman.

SCOTTISH COUNCIL FOR RESEARCH IN EDUCATION (1963) *The Scottish Scholastic Survey—1953* London: University of London Press.

SCOTTISH COUNCIL FOR RESEARCH IN EDUCATION (1968) *Rising Standards in Scottish Primary Schools 1953/1963* London: University of London Press.

WEST, P. V. (1927) *Changing Practice in Handwriting Instruction* Bloomington, Ill.: Public School Publishing Co.